Contents

History of Cameras   2

Fun Ideas with Photos   11

The Important Parts   18

Make a Camera Obscura   25

History of

Cameras!

There are lots and lots of kinds of cameras.
There are cameras that you use to take photographs.
There are video cameras.
There are television cameras.
There are cameras that look out into space.
Did you know that the first camera
was called the camera obscura?

Cameras

Written by Sandy McKay
Illustrated by Trevor Pye

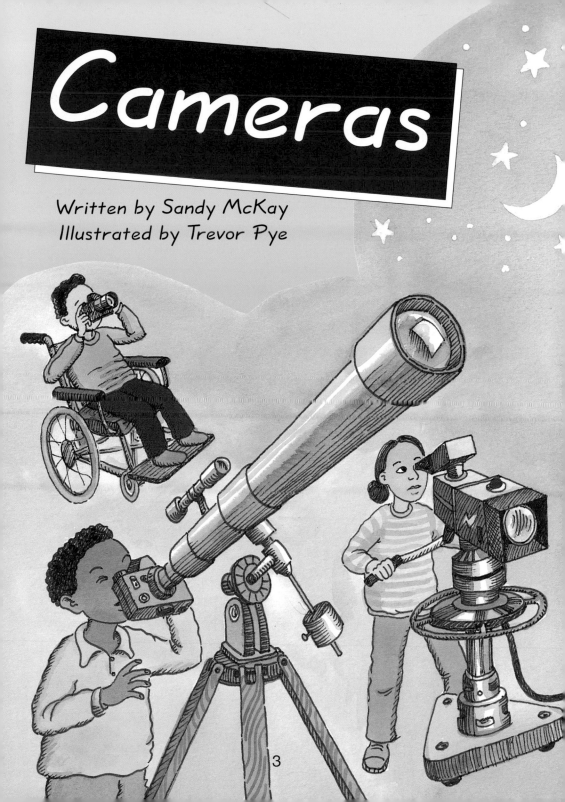

The First Camera

Did you know that camera means "room" and obscura means "dark"?

The first camera
was called the camera obscura.
This camera did not look like
a camera we use today.
This camera was just a darkroom.
People used the darkroom to look at the sun.
They could look at the sun out of a little hole
in the wall and not hurt their eyes.

Then people found out
that they could use the darkroom
to see other things
when the sun was shining.
The little hole in the wall
would let the sunlight
come into the darkroom.
The light would fall onto a wall.
People could look at the wall
and see what was outside.

4

Some people used the darkroom
to help them draw pictures.
They would put some paper
on one of the walls.
The light would hit the paper.
And on the paper
was an upside down picture
of what was outside.
Then they could trace
the picture onto the paper.
This helped them draw a picture.

Making the Camera Better

People wanted to take the camera obscura
with them so that they could see other things.
Sometimes they made the camera
into a table.

Sometimes they made the
camera into a tent.

What do you
now know about the
development of
the camera?

They put a lens from a telescope
in the camera.
This made the picture clear and bright.
They put a mirror
in the camera, too.
Now the picture was the right way up.
Some people put a sheet of glass
at the top of the camera.
They put tracing paper on the glass
so that they could trace the picture.

shade hood

mirror

lens

Making Pictures Stick

People liked to use the camera obscura to trace pictures.
But they wanted to make the picture stick to the paper.
So they put a sheet of metal in their camera.
They put something on the sheet of metal
that turned black when the sun hit it.
They left it in the sun for eight hours
and then they got a picture.

Can you find out what they put on the sheet of metal?

Someone found a way to stop
the camera paper from going dark
when they looked at it in the light.
This meant that the pictures became fixed.

Photographs are "drawings" with light.

8

Cameras Today

Now there are lots of cameras.
There are cameras that take photographs
under the water.

Some cameras can take photographs
of things that are far away.

Some cameras can take photographs
of tiny little things.
Photography is everywhere!

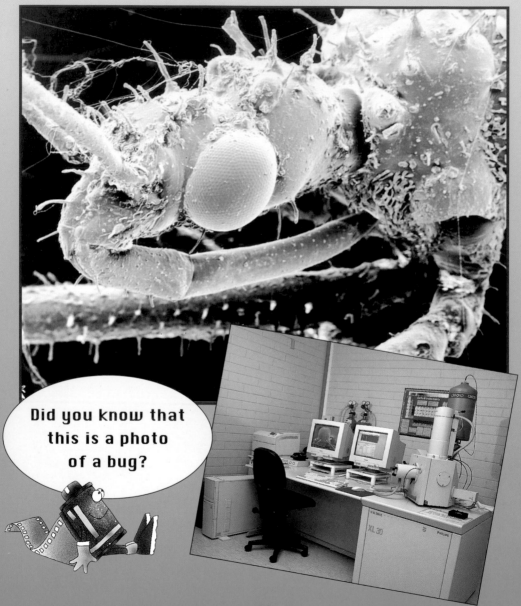

Did you know that
this is a photo
of a bug?

Fun Ideas with Photos

Written by Ann-Marie Heffernan

Today photos are in lots of places.
You can see photos in books.
You can see photos on television.
You can see photos in newspapers,
magazines, and on billboards.
Have you ever taken photos?
If you have, what did you do with them?
Here are some things that you can do with your photos.

IT ALL HAPPENS IN THE BIG CITY

Make a Panorama

Take some photos
of a place that is too big for one photo.
Or you can take some photos
of a friend.
Match your photos up.
The photos can be different shapes, too.
Then you have a panorama!

13

Guess the Photo

Take some photos
of just parts of things.
Get your friends to guess what it is.

You can find out what these are at the bottom of the page.

1. zebra 2. tortoise 3. basketball 4. giraffe

14

Make Your Own Card

Give your friend a card.
Make the card out of your photo.
Write a note to your friend on the card.

Sorry!
I missed your
birthday.

Get well
soon and
come back
to school!

Make a Montage

Make a funny montage out of some old photos.
Cut parts out of each photo,
or put some photos together.
You can overlap some of the photos.
You can put a photograph behind it, too.
Now you have a funny montage!

What name would you give this animal?

The Important Parts

Written by Erin Howard
Illustrated by Nina Price

My mother loves her camera.
But the pictures she takes
are so bad.
She leaves out the important parts.

Look at this picture.
It has a trampoline at the bottom.
It has six feet at the top.
Jordan and Ernesta and I were jumping.
But you can't see Jordan, Ernesta, and me.
My mother left us out.

Look at this picture.
This is our cat.
She is out in the sun.
But you can't see
that she is on the bird table.
You can't see that the birds
can't get to the bird food.
My mother left them out.

What can the mother do to make her pictures better?

Here is a picture of our dog.
He is howling.
Do you know why
our dog is howling?
No. You can't see why.
Our dog howls when Jordan sings.
But you can't see Jordan.
My mother left him out.

This is a picture of Ernesta.
She looks happy.
Do you know why she is happy?
No. You can't see why.
It is Ernesta's birthday.
But you can't see the presents
and the birthday cake.
My mother left them out.

Here is a picture of Jordan.
He looks mad.
Do you know why
he is mad?
No. You can't see why.
Our dog pushed him over.
But you can't see our dog.
My mother left him out.

This picture is taken in the snow.
Jordan and Ernesta are playing in the snow.
Our dog is jumping up and down.
Is this a good picture?
Has it got all the important parts?
Yes. That's because I took it!

What kinds
of things make
a good picture?

Make a Camera Obscura

Written by Sandy McKay   Photographed by Sarah Irvine

To make a camera obscura you will need

A little cardboard box (shoebox)
Tape
Tracing paper
A ruler
Scissors
Thick paper
A pencil

If you aren't very good with scissors, make sure a grown-up is close by.

1. Cut a large rectangle
   out of one side of the box.

2. Cut a piece of tracing paper
   to fit over the rectangle.

3. Tape the tracing paper over the hole.

Can you remember why people used tracing paper on their cameras?

4. Cut out a little hole at the other end of the box.

Why do you need the little hole?

5. Cut out a square piece of thick paper.
It should be bigger than the hole in the box.

6. Make a hole in the middle of the thick paper
with your pencil.

7. Put the thick paper
over the little hole in the box.
Tape up all the sides of the thick paper
so it sticks to the box.

If you don't use a mirror, then your picture will not be the right way up.

8. Now you can take
your camera obscura outside.
Find something to look at
and then hold your camera up to the sun.
Look at the picture on the tracing paper.
Now you can trace your picture.
But don't press too hard,
or you will rip
the paper.

The picture that you see
through the pinhole
on your camera obscura
will not be the right way up.

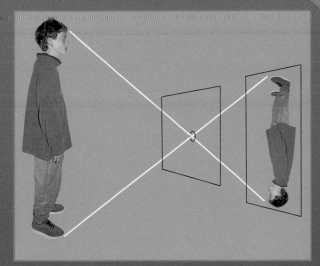

This is what
you see with
your eye.

This is what you see on
the tracing paper on your
camera obscura.

Index

camera obscura   2, 4, 6
cameras
   history of   2, 4–8
   modern   9–10
close-up photographs   14

dark room   4, 5
different kinds of cameras   9

lens   7

making a camera obscura   25–31
   lens   7
   mirror   7
   sheet of glass   7
   tracing paper   7
making a panorama   12
montage   16

panorama   12
photographs
   as cards   15
   fun ideas with 11, 12, 14, 15, 16
   important parts of   18–24

taking photographs   18–24
   taking photographs of
   small things   10
   taking photographs
   underwater   9
   television cameras   2

upside down picture   5, 31

video cameras   2